TV Hospital

The Spirals Series

Fiction

Jim Alderson
Crash in the Jungle
The Witch Princess

Penny Bates
Tiger of the Lake

Jan Carew
Footprints in the Sand
Voices in the Dark

Susan Duberley
The Ring

John Goodwin
Ghost Train

Angela Griffiths
Diary of a Wild Thing
Stories of Suspense

Anita Jackson
The Actor
The Austin Seven
Bennet Manor
Dreams
The Ear
A Game of Life and Death
No Rent to Pay

Paul Jennings
Maggot

Richard Kemble
Grandmother's Secret

Helen Lowerson
The Biz

Margaret Loxton
The Dark Shadow

Bill Ridgway
The Hawkstone
Mr Punch

John Townsend
Back on the Prowl
A Minute to Kill
Night Beast
Snow Beast

Plays

Jan Carew
Computer Killer

Chris Culshaw
Radio Riff-Raff

Angela Griffiths
TV Hospital
Wally and Co.

Paul Groves
Tell Me Where it Hurts

Anita Jackson
The Good, the Bad and the Bungle

Bill Ridgway
Monkey Business

John Townsend
A Bit of a Shambles
Books and Crooks
Clogging the Works
Cowboys, Jelly and Custard
Gulp and Gasp
Hiccups and Slip-ups
Jumping the Gun
A Lot of Old Codswallop
Murder at Muckleby Manor

David Walke
Package Holiday

Non-fiction

Chris Culshaw
Dive into Danger

David Orme
Hackers

Jill Ridge
Lifelines

Bill Ridgway
Lost in Alaska
Over the Wall

Julie Taylor
Lucky Dip

John Townsend
Burke and Hare: The Body Snatchers
Kingdom of the Man-eaters

NEW Spirals PLAYS

TV Hospital

Angela Griffiths

Text © Angela Griffiths 2002

The right of Angela Griffiths to be identified as author of this work has been asserted by her in accordance with the Copyright, Designs and Patents Act 1988.

All rights reserved. No part of this publication may be reproduced or transmitted in any form or by any means, electronic or mechanical, including photocopy, recording or any information storage and retrieval system, without permission in writing from the publisher or under licence from the Copyright Licensing Agency Limited, 90 Tottenham Court Road, London W1T 4LP.

Any person who commits any unauthorised act in relation to this publication may be liable to criminal prosecution and civil claims for damages.

Published in 2002 by:
Nelson Thornes Ltd
Delta Place
27 Bath Road
CHELTENHAM
GL53 7TH
United Kingdom

02 03 04 05 06 / 10 9 8 7 6 5 4 3 2 1

A catalogue record for this book is available from the British Library

ISBN 0-7487-6683-9

Cover illustration by John Harman
Page make-up by Tech-Set, Gateshead

Printed in Croatia by Zrinski

Contents

A play of three acts for four parts, set in a hospital.

Zooming in on the General Ward _____ 6

Close-up in the Operating Theatre _____ 15

Panning Around in the Kitchen _____ 22

Cast in order of appearance

Bud Ivory	A famous TV presenter
Ron Reckit	A patient
Rita Reckit	His wife
Rosie Reckit	His daughter
Nurse	Dr Lush's assistant
Dr Lush	A top woman surgeon
Mr Portly	A patient
Chef	The cook
Matt	A catering student
Meg	Another catering student

Zooming in on the General Ward

4 parts: Bud
           Ron
           Rita
           Rosie

Scene: The general ward of Pexby Hospital. Bud Ivory, the famous TV presenter, is about to start a programme. He has his cameraman, Big Boris, with him.

Bud	We need to start so look sharp, Boris. Get some good shots. Okay? Here we go then. [*To camera*] Hello! We're here in the general ward of Pexby Hospital. Today I'm meeting the odd patient – and here's one. Good morning, what's your name?
Ron	I'm Ron Reckit. I say, are we going out live?
Bud	Well, I hope we're not going out dead! Ha ha!
Ron	No, I mean, is this live TV?
Bud	Not quite. Today we're doing the filming. Then tomorrow we'll be in the studio for edits. You'll be able to see the programme next week. It'll be a fly-on-the-wall documentary.

Ron	What's that?
Bud	It's where we film everything and show it all. Act normal. Think of me as just a fly on the wall.
Ron	Then buzz off!
Bud	Now Ron, I must say you look very well – apart from the leg. That plaster looks heavy. Those wires must be strong. Boris, get a close-up of Ron's plaster and his blue toes.
Ron	I'm fed up. I hate having my leg stuck up in the air like this. I feel like a rocket ready for take-off.
Bud	How long have you been here?
Ron	Ten weeks.
Bud	Ten weeks! That seems a long time for a broken leg.
Ron	Oh, I didn't have a broken leg when I first came in. I only came in with a spare rib.
Bud	A spare rib? I didn't know people had those.
Ron	I haven't now. They took it out.
Bud	If it's not a rude question . . . where was it?
Ron	In my throat.
Bud	Wow, that's a funny place to have a spare rib.
Ron	There's nothing funny about it. It hurt like mad.
Bud	Were you born with it?
Ron	Don't be daft. I sneezed.

Bud	You sneezed and a rib went up to your throat?
Ron	No. I sneezed at the barbecue and it went down whole. That's how I got a spare rib stuck in my throat. With spicy sauce and half a sausage.
Bud	Nasty! But how did that give you a bad leg?
Ron	The nurses made me have a bath, and I slipped on the soap and broke my leg!
Bud	Ha ha! At least it was a clean break.
Ron	Oh good. Here comes my wife, Rita. She's with our girl, Rosie.

[*Rita and Rosie arrive with a big bag of chips*]

Bud	Quick, Boris. Get a good shot of the wife – she's a dish!
Rita	[*Giving Ron a hug*] Hello Ron, my sweetie pie. Sorry we're late. How are you? Oh dear, you look a bit pale and droopy . . . a bit green round the gills. I don't like the way you look at all.
Ron	I don't like the way you look either, Rita. Those leather trousers are much too tight. And that off-the-shoulder blouse is off the planet! Look, we're being filmed. That's Boris the cameraman. He doesn't say much. And this is Bud. He says too much.
Rita	Bud Ivory! I know you! Well, I feel I know you. I've seen you on telly lots of times! Fancy! Just fancy! I can't believe it. Here you are in the flesh!

Rosie	And lots of flesh, too!
Ron	Bud is making a programme about this hospital. He wants us to act normal.
Rosie	That'll be hard.
Bud	Rita, dear, don't lean near the camera like that. Don't keep patting your hair. Just pretend the camera isn't there.
Rita	Right. But I wish I'd known about this TV lark. I'd have put on extra lip gloss.
Rosie	[*Handing over the bag of chips*] Here you are, Dad. It's what you asked for. Chips to cheer you up.
Ron	Did you remember the pickled eggs?
Rosie	No. But that's a really big bag of chips. Do you want a bite of my spare rib?
Ron	Not likely! I'll put the chips under my pillow to keep them warm. I'll enjoy them later when you've all gone home.
Bud	Boris, quick. Get a close-up of the chips.
Ron	Is Boris happy in his work? He seems a bit grumpy.
Bud	He wants a chip. But we're here to talk about you, Ron. For a start, what's the food like in this place?
Ron	It's awful! They think if they make the food nice, nobody will go home.

Bud	Do you enjoy being in this ward?
Rosie	Dad hates being in this ward. Go on, Dad. Tell him.
Ron	Well, the main problem is the others in here. Last week a new man came in. He gave his measles to half the ward before he went home.
Bud	That was a bit rash.
Ron	And you see that bloke over there?
Bud	You mean the one wearing the blue hairnet? Boris, get a long shot of the man in the net!
Ron	Yes, him. He's got Rhyme Disease. He always talks in rhyme. And I'm sure it's catching! All the doctors wear masks and wet suits when they go near him. The nurses give him his food on a long pole. His wife only looks at him through the window.
Bud	Wow! What sort of things does he say?
Ron	Well, he says things like 'I've got a single shingle – it doesn't half tingle!'
Rita	And yesterday he was eating a meat pie and we heard him say 'Big fat fly, get out of my pie! Quick, nurse, quick! I feel quite sick!'
Bud	A fly in hospital? Where did it come from?
Ron	From a fly-on-the-wall documentary!

Rita	Boris – can you get a quick flash of my nice new earrings? Then I can say 'as seen on TV'.
Rosie	And I've got a stud.
Ron	You what?
Rosie	In my eyebrow.
Ron	I told you not to have it done.
Rita	It's not her fault, Ron. She was in the pub last night and sat too near the dartboard. It looks nice.
Bud	What was that noise?
Ron	It's him at the end of the ward. He keeps us all awake at night. He shouts in his sleep. He cries out 'No! No! No!'
Rita	But sometimes he says 'Yes! Yes! Yes!'
Rosie	If only he'd make up his mind.
Bud	Can the doctors do anything?
Ron	Yes. They give sleeping pills. Not to him, the rest of us. They had to wake me up last night to give me mine.
Bud	Wow! Get a shot of that man, Boris.
Ron	When I got back to sleep last night I had a bad dream. I dreamt there was a vulture perched on my bed.
Rita	I hope it wasn't an omen.

Ron	No, I'm sure it was a vulture.
Rosie	Dad, I've just written something on your plaster.
Ron	Oh no! What have you put?
Rosie	I've put 'Don't worry, Dad. It's only one leg. You've still got a spare. To go with your spare rib!'
Bud	Boris! Get a close-up of this plaster. Er, excuse me Rita, try not to stick your face quite so close to the camera. And don't flutter your lashes like that. You look – oh, what's the word?
Ron	Stupid. That's the word.
Rita	I look like a film star. Is that what you mean, Bud?
Bud	Well . . .
Rita	The camera doesn't lie. It'll show my real beauty.
Ron	Listen, I think you should all go home now. I need some peace. And I want to eat my chips. [*He reaches into his bedside locker*] I'll just get my salt and vinegar out ready.
Bud	Careful, Ron! The locker is on wheels.
Rita	Ron, watch out! Your wires are at full stretch!
Rosie	You're spilling your chips, Dad!

  [*The locker suddenly shoots away from Ron's bed*]

Ron	I'm . . . AAAAH!

  [*There is a terrible crash as Ron falls out of bed*]

Bud	Oh, that was great stuff! Boris, I hope you got that on camera! You didn't? Oh no! Ron, do you think you could fall out of bed again?
Ron	Are you mad?
Rita	Oh, Ron! You hit the floor so hard! You'd better stay still. Whatever you do, don't move!
Ron	I wish I could move. Rosie, will you stop pulling those wires!
Rosie	Look, Dad, your chips are all over the floor.
Bud	[*To camera*] Yes, folks, this is a moving story of how a hungry man copes when the chips are down.
Rosie	What a waste of money.
Ron	[*Groaning*] Ooh, ouch! The pain! It's stinging, it's stabbing, it's throbbing.
Bud	Quick, Boris. Get a close-up of Ron's face. Show the agony.
Rita	Oh Ron, poor Dad – you're pale and bad! Your leg looks worse – I'll call the nurse.
Rosie	Hey Mum! I think you've caught Rhyme Disease.
Rita	What, what, what? Don't talk rot.
Bud	Boris, pan in on Rita. Go on, Rita, smile. You're a poet, and you don't know it.

13

Rita	Poor Ron is lame – now I've got fame. I've read the books – I've got the looks. I'm strong and fit – poor Ron's a twit. My name is Rita . . .
Bud	[*Winks to the camera*] You'd love to meet her!
Rita	You cheeky chap – you need a slap! [*She swats Bud with a newspaper*]
Bud	Ow! What's that for?
Ron	You told us to treat you like a fly on the wall. In our house we always swat flies with the paper. Ha! Aaah, it hurts when I laugh.
Rosie	Dad, when you fell out of bed I heard a crack.
Ron	I know. I think I've cracked a rib.
Rosie	Can't you get a spare one? You can always ask for your spare rib back!
Bud	Boris, use the wide-angle lens. Show Ron on the floor with his loved ones round him. [*To camera*] Well, viewers, there you have it. This poor man is down on his luck. He hasn't a leg to stand on, but I won't rib him about it! Do look in again soon. This is Bud Ivory saying bye for now. Do keep safe – and, whatever you do, stay out of hospital!

Close-up in the Operating Theatre

4 parts: Bud
　　　　　Nurse
　　　　　Dr Lush
　　　　　Mr Portly

Scene: The hospital operating theatre. Bud Ivory, the TV presenter, likes to be where the action is. He is about to look in on an operation.

Bud	Nurse, my cameraman needs extra lights. Is it all right if we use this plug?
Nurse	Fine. Go ahead.
Bud	Cheers. I'll just get rid of this plug in the way. [*He pulls it out. There's a high bleep.*] Oh no. What have I done? Sorry. Oh no!
Nurse	Don't worry.
Bud	But I think I've shut down a life support machine. I've killed someone. I've switched them off! What will the doctor say?
Nurse	She may be a bit cross.
Bud	Can't she do something?

15

Nurse	She'll just have to look untidy. She likes to look at her best for operations. You switched off her heated hair rollers.
Bud	Phew! Right Boris, start the camera. [*To camera*] Hello! Yes, it's me, Bud Ivory. Welcome to Pexby Hospital. As you can see, today we're in the operating theatre. First, let's meet Dr Lush. She's young, she's lovely, and she's fast.
Dr Lush	But my hair's a mess. Are you all scrubbed up and ready?
Bud	Yes. But let me tell you, I'm nervous. Very nervous. I hope there won't be too much blood and guts.
Dr Lush	Bud, this is an operating theatre, not a garden party. If the blood spurts, just step aside. Now, where's our first patient?
Nurse	He's outside, all ready. I'll just bring the trolley in.
Bud	Here he comes. Quick, Boris, get a close-up shot of his face. Show the fear.
Nurse	Welcome, Mr Portly.
Mr Portly	It's a bit bright in here.
Dr Lush	Hi, Mr Portly! What's that funny noise?
Mr Portly	It's my teeth. I'm scared.
Bud	Boris, do a close-up of the teeth!

Nurse	Mr Portly, you've struck lucky. Today we're being filmed for TV! Look, this is Bud Ivory, the famous presenter.
Bud	Hi there, Mr Portly! I'm glad I'm not in your shoes – I mean bed socks. Perhaps you saw the film I made last year? It was called Messy Medical Mistakes.
Mr Portly	Oh dear.
Dr Lush	Right, let's get on. What sort of operation are we doing?
Nurse	Mr Portly needs his stomach looking into. He says he gets a funny feeling in it.
Mr Portly	Yes, like butterflies.
Dr Lush	Very common. Right, nurse. Is everything ready? Scalpel? Swabs? Scissors? Butterfly net?
Nurse	All ready.
Dr Lush	Oh . . . wait a minute. I'm feeling peckish. I'll just make a start on my cheese rolls. I hope nobody minds if I munch while I work. I missed breakfast this morning.
Bud	But Doc, surely you can't eat while you're operating. What about germs?
Dr Lush	I'll just have to take the risk and hope I don't catch anything. [*Munch, munch*]

Bud	I mean, what about germs from your rolls?
Dr Lush	Don't talk daft. I always buy my rolls from a very clean shop.
Nurse	Right, Mr Portly. We're going to put you out now.
Mr Portly	Er – I think I'd like a second opinion.
Dr Lush	Okay. You've also got dandruff and bad breath.
Mr Portly	But I feel bad. It's the sight of all that blood.
Dr Lush	We haven't started yet. That's just ketchup from my roll. Now, how do you want to be put to sleep? Will it be gas or the wooden mallet?
Mr Portly	W-w-what do you mean?
Dr Lush	It's the latest idea for saving money. If I were you, I'd choose gas. That's if we've got a coin for the meter.
Nurse	Yes, I've got 20p. Will it be enough?
Dr Lush	Plenty. I'll have to be extra quick.
Nurse	Right, pop the tube in your mouth, Mr Portly. Oops, it's blocked with bits of cheese. Here goes then. Breathe deeply, Mr Portly. That's the way. Nice deep breaths.
Bud	Boris, get a good shot of this. It's high drama. The viewers will love it.
Mr Portly	Hold on, I've changed my mind. I don't think I want this op . . . ZZZZZZ.

Dr Lush   He's out. Let's start. Nurse, hand me the scalpel.

Bud   Oh dear! [*To camera*] Nervous viewers should look away now. Oooh, I'm going to look away too, in case I faint . . . Boris, you keep filming. We could be just a heartbeat away from the gas running out.

Nurse   Don't worry, Bud. If you faint, I'll revive you with the kiss of life. I'm dead keen to practise it.

Dr Lush   There . . . I've opened up. The patient is still breathing. Just. Now, let's see what we have here. Yes . . . it all looks quite normal. Liver, kidneys, spleen, camshaft . . .

Bud   Camshaft?

Dr Lush   This is major surgery, Bud.

Bud   Doc, perhaps you can lift something out for the camera . . . Boris, go in close. Closer. Closer. Oh, not that close! Now you'll have to wipe the lens.

Mr Portly   Oooh! Oooh! Ooh-wah! Doopy doopy doo-wah!

Bud   I think he's coming round.

Dr Lush   That gas is running out. Quick, nurse – use the wooden mallet!

Nurse   [*Clonk!*] There, he's out for the count.

Dr Lush   I'd better sew him up quickly, before he comes round again. Nurse, hand me that reel of cotton. I hope the camera can pick this up. I'm a dab hand at cross-stitch.

Bud	Boris, pan round and come in for a nice close-up. [*To camera*] Viewers, look at this. Dr Lush is faster than a sewing machine.
Nurse	Right, we seem to be finished. Can I clear things away now, doctor?
Dr Lush	Yes – but hold on a minute. Where's my other cheese roll? I only ate one.
Nurse	Oh no! Dr Lush, I've just had a horrid thought.
Dr Lush	Well, keep it to yourself. Help me find my missing roll.
Nurse	Dr Lush, I think your cheese roll got packed into the patient. You were so quick with the sewing up, we didn't spot it.
Dr Lush	Oh no!
Bud	We'll have it all on film.
Mr Portly	Oooh . . . oooh . . . Where am I?
Dr Lush	How are you, Mr Portly? How do you feel?
Mr Portly	I feel a bit full . . . and cheesy . . . er, I mean squeezy. No, I mean queasy. What do I mean? Ha ha! Tee hee! Ha ha!
Bud	He seems pretty happy.
Dr Lush	That's the gas. Gas always makes you giggle.
Bud	Not me. It makes me cry. Mainly when I get the gas bill!

Mr Portly	I feel all funny inside. Did the operation go well?
Nurse	Nothing to worry about, Mr Portly. We got in a bit of a pickle at one point.
Mr Portly	Yes, I can see it. Pickle, cheese and ketchup. It's all over my chest.
Bud	Crumbs!
Nurse	Really? I thought I'd brushed them off.
Dr Lush	Oops. That's not ketchup! Quick, pass me a roll.
Nurse	Are you still peckish?
Dr Lush	Not a cheese roll. A kitchen roll. For the blood.
Bud	[*To camera*] Well, viewers, as Mr Portly rolls about in stitches, we'll leave the nurse to mop up the ... ketchup oozing over his chest. [*There's a loud crash*] Oh no! Boris our cameraman has fainted. With the nurse leaping on him to give the kiss of life, this is Bud Ivory saying bye for now. Take care – and, whatever you do, stay out of hospital!

Panning Around in the Kitchen

4 parts: Bud
          Chef
          Matt
          Meg

Scene: The busy hospital kitchen where hundreds of meals are cooked every day. Bud Ivory, the TV presenter, is in the thick of it.

Bud	Are we ready for the filming to start?
Chef	Yes. I've got my best white jacket and high hat.
Matt	You look like a real top chef.
Meg	I think you should give your trousers a check.
Chef	They've already got a check. Look. Black and white, like a chess board.
Meg	No, I mean give them a check. They're undone.
Bud	Right, Boris, start filming . . . ready, steady, cook . . . I mean, go. Get a full shot of me as I do the intro.
Matt	We're going to be on telly!

Bud	[*To camera*] Hello! Here we are in Pexby Hospital. I'm Bud Ivory, your presenter. Today we're in the hospital kitchen. Just look at this long table covered with soggy sprouts. Now let's meet the man in charge. Hi.
Chef	[*In a very high voice*] Hello!
Bud	CUT! Why did you speak in a squeaky voice?
Chef	I thought you said 'high'.
Bud	Boris, start again. Here we have two students from catering college.
Matt	Hi. I'm Matt.
Meg	And I'm Meg. We're here on our NVQ.
Bud	Right, Chef, tell me what's going on here.
Chef	We're just chopping spuds. Ready for lunch.
Bud	Boris, get a long shot of this pile of potato peelings. Now, Chef, tell us what tasty treat is on the menu today.
Chef	Soup with crusty bread.
Bud	Yummy! But do let me help in some way. It looks like hard work.
Matt	Very.
Meg	Thanks, Bud. Here's a scalpel. You can chop the onions.
Bud	Don't you have machines in this kitchen?

Matt	Yes. Us. Slaves. Cheap labour.
Bud	While I work, can I ask Chef a question?
Chef	Just one question then. Go on.
Bud	Chef, why do you wear such a large gold earring? And why do you have chewing gum stuck in your beard? And why are you wearing odd socks? And why do you have a red hanky in your top pocket?
Chef	I'm good at maths. That's not ONE question. I'll answer just one. My red hanky is to mop my brow. It gets hot in here. I brought it back from India.
Matt	Chef likes to travel a lot.
Meg	He always brings things back. See that huge green lizard up on that wall? He brought that back from Brazil last year.
Bud	Boris, pan in on that. It looks gross.
Chef	It often falls into the salad. It takes us weeks to find it again.
Matt	And you see that very old fork up there? It's Roman. He picked that up in Bath.
Bud	Boris, get that. Zoom in on that sign on the handle. Just a minute . . . it says 'NHS'. That's not Roman. Where in Bath did you find it?
Chef	It was just by the soap and I sat on it.

Bud	Boris, pan round. Show the lot.
Chef	Don't show the floor! It's a mess. Spots of grease. We've been too busy to clean up. I've only just come back from China.
Bud	Why do you travel so much?
Chef	Well, Bud, I travel for the sake of this hospital.
Matt	You can take that with a pinch of salt!
Chef	I like to get ideas, you see. When I come back from another country, I always bring a new recipe. I took away a lot from China.
Meg	Yeah – a Chinese takeaway.
Matt	Nice wok if you can get it!
Chef	Last month we had a Sample Sushi day.
Meg	It was just raw fish and chips.
Chef	The month before that we had a Go Greek day.
Matt	That was fish and chips with an olive.
Chef	Then there was the Fantastic French day.
Meg	Fish and chips with snails from the hospital flowerbed.
Bud	Plenty of wine?
Matt	You bet – everyone did. Whine, whine, whine all day!
Bud	[*Sniffing*] Oh dear.

Meg	Bud, are you crying because you feel sorry for the patients?
Chef	Do you want to use my red silk hanky?
Bud	No, it's only the onions making me cry.
Matt	We cry most days. We work our fingers to the bone.
Meg	Chef can't get the staff.
Chef	Right, you lot. Get these spuds in the pot. It's almost up to the boil.
Bud	Wow! What a huge cooking pot! Get a shot of this, Boris. Pan in on the pan.
Chef	It holds sixty litres of soup.
Bud	Sixty litres! Hey, it's dripping out the bottom.
Chef	That's right. It's LEEK soup.
Meg	Tip the onions in, Bud. Don't splash.

[*They tip the lot into the pot*]

Chef	There, that's done. Now I'll give it all a stir with my long spoon. It'll be ready just in time for lunch.
Bud	What's on the menu for this evening?
Chef	Curried meat balls with rice.
Bud	From Asia?
Matt	No, from Asda.

Meg	Chef, we have a small problem. I've just found half a slug. Can we do anything?
Matt	Send for a nurse? Take it to A and E? Put a plaster on it?
Bud	Boris, quick with the camera! Close-up. Half a slug!
Chef	It means the other half has gone into the soup!
Bud	YUK!
Chef	These things happen. This is a busy place. Phew! I'm hot. I need to mop my brow. Where's my red hanky? Would someone stir the soup for me?
Meg	Yes, I'll do it. [*Busy stirring*] Oh Chef, you'd better come and see. The soup looks odd. It's turning pink.
Chef	PINK?
Meg	Yes. Pink and frothy. It's getting pinker by the minute.
Matt	Look, Chef! There's your red hanky in the soup. I'll fish it out.
Meg	Oh heck! What will you do now, Chef?
Chef	I'll have to use my sleeve to mop my brow.
Meg	No, I mean what will you do about the soup?
Chef	Let me think a minute.

Bud	Boris, quick. Get a close-up of this pink soup.
Chef	I know what to do. I need herbs. Lots of herbs.
Matt	Right, here's basil and sage.
Meg	And here's parsley and dill.
Chef	Have you got the thyme?
Bud	Yeah, it's half past ten.
Meg	I'll add a few litres of ketchup. That should do the trick. Now we must think of a new name for it. It's gone a yucky brown.
Matt	Call it Spicy Mud Soup.
Meg	I know! Let's call it after Bud. Bud Mud Soup!
Chef	HEY! I hope you haven't got all this mess on film.
Bud	You bet. People love to watch disasters.
Chef	But . . . but . . .
Bud	You'll be famous. The whole world will see how to make Bud Mud Soup.
Chef	Get out!
Bud	[*To camera*] Well, we've really seen the hidden side of a hospital kitchen. I'll go over to the soup . . . AAAAAAH!

[*Bud slips on some grease and falls over*]

Matt	Bud, are you all right?

Bud   No. I banged my head. Now I'm seeing stars. Ooh.

Matt   Don't move, Bud. Just lie back. Seeing stars is a bad sign.

Chef   Bud Ivory, star of TV, sees stars!

Meg   I've rung A and E. They're sending a stretcher.

Bud   OH NO! BORIS! You're not filming this, are you? Boris, I beg you! Please don't show me being carted away on a stretcher. [*To camera*] Well, viewers, I may be down but I'm not out. Ooh, ouch! This is Bud Ivory, your best TV presenter, fading out fast. Bye for now. Keep well. Keep safe. And do stay out of hospital! Cut. CUT. Not that . . . AAAAH!